THE BIRD AND THE ELEPHANT

PHILOSOPHY FOR YOUNG MINDS

BY DOMINIC SMITH

Dominic Smith
London, UK.

Email: thesunwasjustmagic@gmail.com

Web: www.thebirdandtheelephant.com

Joseph & Simon Publishing.

ISBN 978-1-5272-0982-4

Cover design by Damonza.
Book design and layout by Peter Gwyer.
Illustrations by Jonathan Duck.
Illustrations editor Tom Mundell.

Dedicated to all inquisitive minds.
Never stop wondering.

Table of Contents

The rock that wasn't a rock   1

Who are we?   4

Where do we come from?   7

Why are we here?   10

Friendship   13

Why do bad things happen?   16

Happiness   20

Morality   23

Destiny   26

Love   29

Philosophy   32

"If you get lost, there's no need to panic. When the bird speaks it's **bold** and when the elephant - it's *italic*."

The rock that wasn't a rock

On a beautiful day, where the sun was just magic
And the sky was so blue, you could reach up and grab it
A Drongo bird was far from his nest.
As he swooped and he soared, he felt like a rest.

So he looked down below and studied the ground
Till a large grey rock he suddenly found.
He adjusted his wings and made his descent,
For a super smooth landing you'd call – excellent!

He stood for some seconds and rested his eyes,
When all of a sudden, to his complete surprise
The rock that he thought was so stable and true
Just started to move, quite out of the blue.

Squawk! said the bird. **What's happening here?**
As the rock continued to wobble and rear.
But it wasn't a rock and it wasn't a stone,
It was an elephant's back that the bird had made home.

Out came some ears and up came a trunk
The bird turned around and now saw from the front.
What is this huge rock that moves when I land?
I'm an elephant, you're a bird and we both share this land.

The bird was surprised, how did he not see?
Now he was wishing he'd aimed for a tree.
He thought about what the elephant said,
He didn't agree and started shaking his head.

We do not share this land for I own the sky
You can't even jump let alone lift up and fly.
But why do you fly? And who made the sky?
What is the true meaning between you and I?

The bird looked confused, who was this old fool
To ask him these questions like some sort of school?
He was slow he was heavy he hadn't seen sights,
While swooping and soaring to marvellous heights.

What are you talking about? asked the bird in a huff.
Life, the universe, that sort of stuff.
Don't you ever ask questions? Discuss them and talk?
My favourite pastime is to eat, think and walk.

The bird was annoyed, he only wanted a rest.
Now it seemed like he'd signed up for some sort of test.
He decided to stop him, this was going too far.
Just who - Mr Elephant - do you think that you are?

Who are we?

Now that's a good question! the elephant declared.
Are you ready for the answer? Are you fully prepared?
The bird said, **Of course, now tell me it's due.**
Well you - are me, and I - am you.

The bird started to laugh, how stupid, he thought
The dumbest elephant alive he'd seem to have caught
That makes no sense; I think I'll be going
Now wait just a second, the proofs in the showing.

Take a deep breath, the elephant said.
The bird inhaled deeply and lifted his head.
The elephant then filled his trunk up with air,
Do you see? That much we both have to share.

Are you thirsty? **A little,** the bird answered back.
The trunk got some water and like the biggest grey tap,
It poured a small puddle on the back of its neck,
And the bird took a drink while the elephant stepped.

Can you feel the sun? **Oh yes,** said the bird
It's a beautiful day to fly and observe.
I feel it too, I'm thirsty, I breathe,
Now can you see it's the same life we lead?

I have dreams and thoughts, thoughts and dreams
Goals and aspirations I wish to achieve.
Fears and doubts, doubts and fears
I cry, you cry. We share the same tears.

The bird fell silent, he thought for quite long.
Then had an idea that'd prove elephant wrong.
There's a thing, you know, that I do in the loo.
Yes, said the elephant. *I do that thing too.*

Oh... said the bird, and he had to agree.
I guess I am like you, and you are like me.
That's right! said the elephant. I'm glad that you see,
So now the real question is, who then - are we?

Where do we come from?

Where do you come from? the elephant said.
That's easy, said the bird. **I come from an egg.**
But before the egg, what about that?
I came from my mother, that's a natural fact.

And before your mother? **I don't understand?**
Where do we all come from? Who built this fine land?
And the stars and the moon, the earth and the sun,
How did it begin? Where was it begun?

Some believe that it's all accidental,
We just popped and appeared from a bang that was central.
And for millions of years we evolved and we grew,
To the point where we now look like me and you.

You and I, said the bird, correcting his speech,
Who despite his small size could still rightly teach.
You and I, said the elephant, sarcasm displaying,
And then he continued with what he was saying.

Some believe that a powerful being
Made us and everything else that we're seeing.
From the mountains and oceans, rivers and seas,
To the humans, the crocodiles, the tigers and bees.

So which one is right, which one is the truth?
It's not quite that simple, like making a tooth.
The question is not which one is the lead,
But simply, which one do you choose to believe?

But what about evidence, there must be a case?
There is, it's the battle of science and faith.
And they've argued their points for a very long time
You read, you learn and your beliefs you design.

But what If I don't want to take either side?
That's fine, you're allowed, you can be your own tide.
You don't have to follow, you don't have to lead,
Life's gift is still yours because you're able to breathe.

Why are we here?

So you are an elephant and you eat grass for your dinner.
I have two wings and I'm a pretty good singer.
Over there's a hyena, she's known for her laugh,
And that thing with the long neck is called a giraffe.

The bird pointed out the things that he saw,
His eyes spotted creatures from the sky to the floor.
Then just like his vision his mind became clear,
And he said to the elephant, **Why are we all here?**

The elephant stopped and chewed on some grass.
He knew that a question so *huge* he'd been asked.
He wanted to answer as best as he could,
So he walked to a tree and he chewed on some wood.

Why are you eating? Did you not hear me speak?
I think even better when I've something to eat.
Just let me finish then I'll answer you clear,
In the meantime, why do you think that we're here?

Well, I am a bird so my role is to fly.
I must be here then to pretty the sky,
Sing in the morning, and build my own nest
And sometimes, like now, my wings need a rest.

The elephant had finally finished his food.
He answered the bird in a serious mood.
What if the reason we're actually here
Is to ask - what is the reason we're here?

The bird squinted his eyes and tilted his head.
His mind was confused, like he'd got out of bed.
Look, said the elephant. *We're talking, discussing,*
Questioning life while the world keeps on rushing.

Maybe our mission while our planet revolves
Is to ask all the questions that are so hard to solve?
Our land is fantastic, so much we can build.
But maybe it's our minds were supposed to have filled.

The bird had a curious look in his eye,
Funny, that's not how I thought you'd reply.
I imagined you'd say 'to befriend one another'
Oh, that's a discussion I'll save for another.

Friendship

A friend is one on whom you can depend
To be there, by your side, to borrow or lend.
To help and advise, from light chats to wise,
Who doesn't change voices or wear a disguise.

Good times or bad, sunshine or monsoon,
A friend is the one that you want to see soon.
A friend won't mock you, or call you bad names
Or test you to do stuff and pretend it's a game.

It's not always easy to find a good friend.
That's why sometimes you must see in the end,
In a world full of strangers and people all new
The first friend you have is actually you.

You know what you like, your favourite tastes
Your favourite game and your favourite place
What makes you feel happy what makes you feel low
What you need deep inside, to help you to grow.

When you realise that, then you're never alone,
And a friend is easy to find when you roam.
Knowing yourself can help you know others
You can see deep inside, like a pot with no cover.

Some count their friends, but friends don't keep score.
I'd rather have one than a hundred and four.
You could have so many friends that they'd fill up a bus!
But what is the point if not one you can trust?

So have good friends and be a good friend,
You be the one on which a person depends.
Treat others as you would like to be treated,
Nobody wants to be hurt or deleted.

To look after each other is simple and true
We all need good friends no matter when, no matter who.
The world needs a friend and we are its closest,
So be that good friend when a new friend approaches.

Why do bad things happen?

I had a cousin who try as he might,
Couldn't quite master the art of good flight.
One day he crash-landed. His wings started shaking.
And before he could get up, a lioness ate him!

He was a good bird, never did anything wrong.
He didn't peck humans or annoy with his song.
So why, for him, did life have to stop?
I still think about him, I miss him a lot.

Now you're thinking like a philosopher.
The questions we ask aren't always popular.
Why do bad things happen to those who aren't bad?
That almost suggests that world is quite mad.

Light and dark, naughty and nice,
There must be a balance to this thing we call life.
And even though many good things you'll discover
You cannot have one, without having the other.

Your cousin was unlucky, it's sad what you feel.
But maybe the lioness was desperate for a meal?
And if she didn't eat she was going to die,
Your cousin saved her life, what a wonderful guy.

There's always two sides, even when you must cry.
When our time runs out, we can't ask - but why?
Just know that the plan is bigger than us.
And eventually, we'll all make our way to the dust.

But after the dust, that's when we'll all see
If there's more life for you, and more life or me.
I believe that there is, some believe that there's not.
Either way I'm excited to see what is what.

As they walked and they talked,
They talked and they walked.
And the elephant shared all the things he'd been taught.
And the bird asked questions, again and again,
While this new information ran all through his brain.

Happiness

The path in life that happiness brings
Is not from buying things and things,
And things and things, more things and things.
If you've only eight fingers, why have twenty rings?

It's hard to live, when some compete,
About who's got the best pair of shoes on their feet.
But you don't wear shoes? the bird declared.
I know, it's the point that I'm trying to share.

A happy mind thinks happy thoughts.
It sounds simple but the truth I've actually caught.
Exactly how happy I want me to be,
Is completely, and utterly, just up to me!

But what if you slip and step on your trunk?
You wouldn't be happy, I bet for a month!
It might hurt a little, I might scream and wail
But then I'd be happy I didn't step on my tail!

What if a monkey, up in a tree,
Started throwing coconuts, and hit you with three?
Then I would shout and tell him to stop!
But be happy he's such a magnificent shot.

I see what you're doing, you're twisting my words
This is not going to work, it's simply absurd.
But it can and it does, for happiness is
Inside you, not behind you, so find it and live.

Peace can be found if you no longer shout,
Stress can be less if you just let it out,
Angers not anger, it's good thoughts gone bad.
So erase all those thoughts, and you're no longer sad.

A billion bananas will never be enough
If I can't be happy with one.
A billion smiles I can give to the world
If I just decide to be fun.

Morality

Have you ever done anyone a helpful favour?
Yes, one time I rescued my neighbour.
She's a mouse, and I saw that a cat was behind her,
So I carried her off where the cat couldn't find her.

But as I landed safely and let her back out,
She was very annoyed, oh didn't she shout.
I thought I was about to get bitten and beaten,
Until I explained that she almost was eaten!

And why did you do it? I felt it was right.
But how did you know? And try as he might,
He could not explain the reason he knew.
It was just a feeling inside. I felt it was true.

This is morality, the difference between right and wrong.
Some say you have to be taught it, some say you know
all along.
You didn't have to help your neighbour in trouble,
You saw and you reacted, super quick, on the double.

It can be described as a compass, pointing out your route.
Sometimes you ignore it, but it always knows the truth.
It's not just for missions and rescuing mice,
It's to help you be better, ensure that you're nice.

If you lived in a tree with ninety-nine birds,
And each one was good, through actions and words,
What a wonderful place that truly would be,
For you, and the rest of the birds in that tree.

But if you lived in a tree with ninety-nine birds
Who were mean and nasty and always got on your
nerves,
What a horrible place that truly would be,
For you, and you'd probably just long to be free.

Well think of that tree as the world that we live in.
Let's make it a good tree with kindness and giving.
Our moral compass always pointing to good.
That's the world I would have if I could.

Destiny

Why did you decide to make my back your home?
From way up there, you looked like a big stone.
And when did you decide to swoop and fly down?
Just a few seconds before I looked at the ground.

Are you sure? Yes I'm sure.
But are you sure? Yes, I'm sure!
But what if I told you every decision you make,
Whether it's clever and wise or a silly mistake,
Might not be impulsive, and for the rest of your days,
All your decisions have already been made.

Already been made?
Already been made
Already been made?
Already been made.

By whom?
By you
By me?
By you.

So you're saying I've already chosen the meal
That I'll eat, in three months' time, in a field.
I'm saying, perhaps, if free will is not free,
That your future is something they call – destiny.

Well my mum still tells me to go take a bath,
So I'm not entirely in control of my path.
No. That's not what I'm trying to say.
When you're bigger and older and all on your way.

Maybe your futures already been written?
Just like a cat must start as a kitten,
Just like the sun must set every night.
You have a story for the rest of your life.

It might be great, amazing and long,
The universe knows, because it composed your song.
So I can do nothing? Stay in bed all day?
If my life's already written, I can just let it play.

No, said the elephant. That's just lazy thinking.
If I didn't go to the river, I'd die from not drinking.
To follow your dreams work is not exempt,
It's whether your dreams have already been dreamt.

This is a tough one, my minds spinning faster.
The elephant smiled. Just think, don't answer.
Two plus two equals four, of that you can be sure,
But these kind of questions require much more.

Love

Love? Oh let's let that subject go missing,
Love is just softness, all hugging and kissing.
I'm not the slightest bit interested in love,
I'm a Drongo bird, not a pretty white dove.

Love is for all, not just the grown and romantic.
Swans fall in love and they're not so gigantic.
Love is just caring, but on an incredible scale.
You can be the tiniest fish, but you can love like a whale.

Well I'll never love. The bird was quite sure.
I don't have the time, I can easily ignore
The other pretty birds with their cute, little smiles
They come over here? I'll fly that way for miles!

Remember the moment you took your first flight?
I do, said the bird, in his mind was the sight.
Well if you had looked back from where you'd just been,
The love in your proud parents eyes you'd have seen.

In fact, even though your two wings were sturdy,
It was their love that carried you on your very first journey.
For love can be given as well as received.
If life is an oak tree then love is the seed.

When all else is gone, and nothing is left,
It's love that I'll say with my very last breath.
You say love's so important, but how can you prove it?
Love is like soap. It works if you use it.

Why must it be love, can't I just 'like it a lot'?
Asked the bird, with indifference, not in love with the plot.
Who do you love? said the bird, quick and blindly.
I love everyone. Even you, said the elephant kindly.

Me? said the bird. **But how? But why?**
I love our conversation, and when you return to the sky
One day you'll remember the talks that we shared,
You'll know that I loved, and in my answers I cared.

Love and be loved, from family to friends,
For you never can tell when the journey will end.
Don't be afraid to open up and be true,
The sweetest sentence on earth is pronounced - I love you.

Philosophy

I think therefore I am,
I speak and also eat,
I must be alive,
I can feel it in my beak!

I think therefore I am,
From sunrise to dusk,
I must be alive,
I can feel it in my tusks!

So philosophy is just talking and sharing ideas,
Trying to find answers with help from our peers,
With logic and reason, thought and debate,
Evidence that's provable and some with no weight.

And after all the possibilities have been thoroughly
discussed,
The final conclusion is still up to us.
We can write our own chapters, from one page to a book.
For thousands to read or not one person to look.

It's personal but open, because all can join in,
It's a race we're all running, without needing to win.
In fact, it's a race that never will stop,
It's fun to take part, I like it a lot.

The elephant smiled he felt very proud.
He was impressed with the bird, but didn't say it aloud.
In fact he felt sad, because he knew it was time
For the bird to be leaving, the sunset was the sign.

But he held it all in and buried his sorrow.
Then the bird simply said, **See you tomorrow?**
The elephant smiled. *That would be great!*
Come by after nine, I wake up at eight.

I go flying at ten. So I'll see you around then,
And we'll talk on some more my wisest new friend.
Then the bird lifted up and took to the sky,
The elephant waved and they both called out, bye.

The sunset was beautiful, the sky was deep red,
What a day, thought the elephant, happy thoughts
filled his head.
What a day, thought the bird, as he flew to his nest,
He knew he'd sleep well, his mind he'd soon rest.

But the bird couldn't wait for the morning to arrive,
So many new questions were filling his mind.
He made it home safely, and sleep came at last.
If you met the elephant, what would you ask?

WRITE YOUR QUESTIONS

Discuss them with your parents, your teachers and your friends.

About the author

Having lived in Brazil, Germany, UK, and Northern Ireland, the now - London based - Dominic, presents his story. Philosophy, at its most basic is your take on life and its biggest and most challenging questions. This is Dominic's take. He hopes it inspires you to think about yours.

Dominic has been interested in poetry and story writing since a young child. This love grew and blossomed into a music career, writing songs and lyrics and performing all over the world. As a soloist he has won Best MC awards in 2014 and 2015, and as part of a band he won the Mercury Prize, a MOBO and a Q award in the late 90s. A career in radio soon followed, hosting a national chart show that kept him close to the music and rhymes he loves.

The 'Bird and the Elephant' was inspired by a simple photo of a bird sat on an elephant's back. This brought forward thoughts about the wonderful conversations they might share together, and that transformed into the work you have just read and hopefully enjoyed.

www.thebirdandtheelephant.com